Mini-sagas

Edited by Sue Hackman

Hodder Murray
A MEMBER OF THE HODDER HEADLINE GROUP

Hodder Headline's policy is to use papers that are natural, renewable and recyclable products and made from wood grown in sustainable forests. The logging and manufacturing processes are expected to conform to the environmental regulations of the country of origin.

Orders: please contact Bookpoint Ltd, 130 Milton Park, Abingdon, Oxon OX14 4SB. Telephone: (44) 01235 827720. Fax: (44) 01235 400454. Lines are open from 9.00am to 5.00pm, Monday to Saturday, with a 24-hour message answering service.
Visit our website at www.hoddereducation.co.uk

Individual mini-sagas © Telegraph Group Limited 1985, 1999
Accompanying text © Sue Hackman 2006
First published in the Hodder Reading Project series in 2006
by Hodder Murray, an imprint of Hodder Education, a member of the Hodder Headline Group, 338 Euston Road, London NW1 3BH.

Impression number   10 9 8 7 6 5 4
Year   2011 2010 2009 2008 2007

All rights reserved. Apart from any use permitted under UK copyright law, no part of this publication may be reproduced or transmitted in any form or by any means, electronic or mechanical, including photocopying and recording, or held within any information storage and retrieval system, without permission in writing from the publisher or under licence from the Copyright Licensing Agency Limited. Further details of such licences (for reprographic reproduction) may be obtained from the Copyright Licensing Agency Limited, Saffron House, 6-10 Kirby Street, London EC1N 8TS.

Cover photo: Cat and goldfish bowl © Cydney Conger/Corbis.
Internal artwork © Barking Dog.
Typeset by Transet Limited, Coventry, England.
Printed in Great Britain by CPI, Bath.

A catalogue record for this title is available from the British Library

ISBN-10: 0 340 91577 3
ISBN-13: 978 0340 915 776

Contents

	Page
Introduction	1
Mini-sagas	2
Cautionary tales	3
Fantasy	7
Oops!	12
Riddles	15
Dreams come true	19
Sting in the tail	22
Answers to the Riddles	26
Acknowledgements	27

Introduction

Not every story is as long as a book.
Not every story takes ages to read.

Here you can find stories that are clever, crafty, well-made and above all – short!

When writers choose to keep it short, they have to squeeze every bit of meaning into a few words, so every word counts. Short art has to be quick and clever and get to the point.

It's not about how long it is; it's the thought that counts.

Mini-sagas

A mini-saga is a story in just 50 words: not a word more, not a word less. But it can have a title of up to 15 words. It must tell a story, not just a joke. It has to have a point.

The mini-saga competition was started by the newspaper the *Daily Telegraph* in 1982. 32,000 people wrote in, even members of the royal family!

Cautionary tales

The first group of mini-sagas are cautionary tales.
This means they act as warnings to the reader.
Cautionary tales show the reader what will happen if they do something bad.

Lifetime

They say that when a man drowns,
his whole life flashes before him.
They also say that some men
seek out that which they fear most.

Thus George became a sailor.

As the sea sucked the ship down
George's terror came true.

While he drowned he had nothing
worth watching.

To love forever

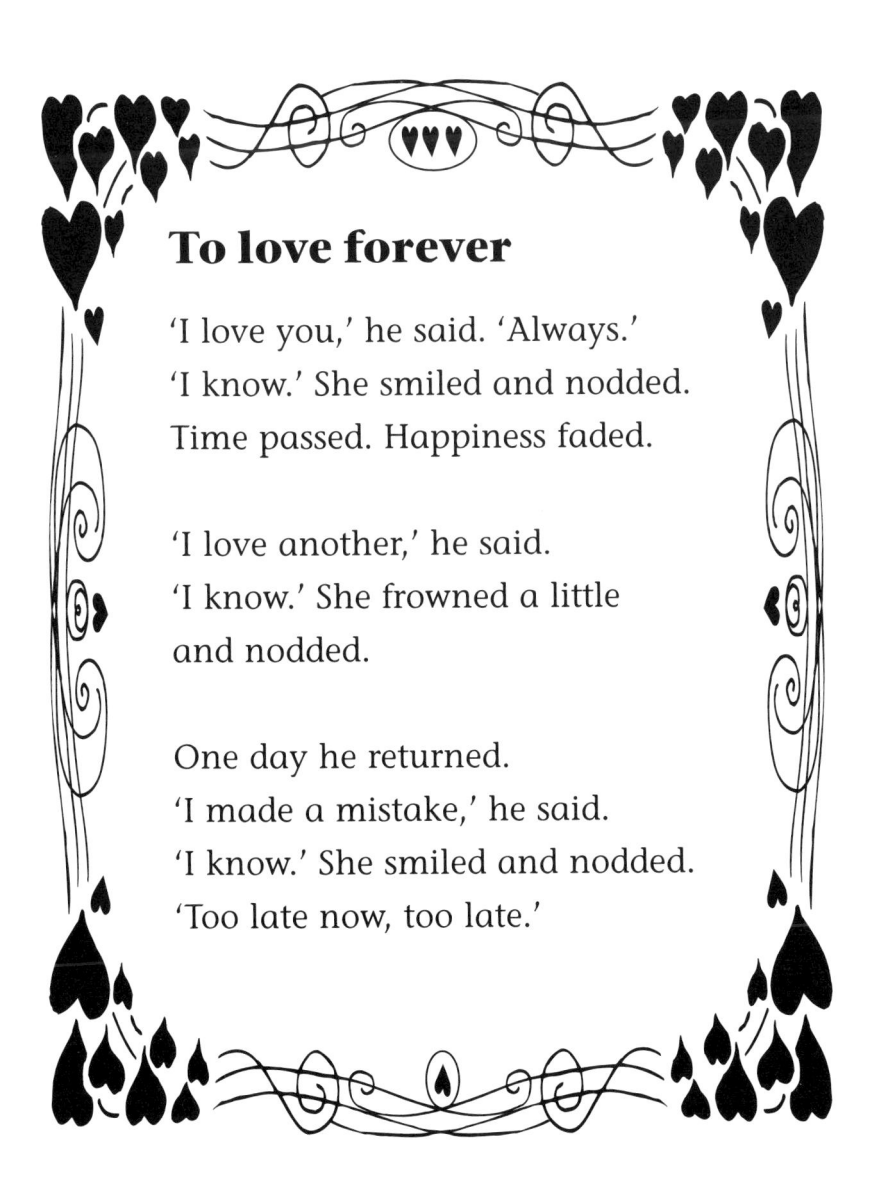

'I love you,' he said. 'Always.'
'I know.' She smiled and nodded.
Time passed. Happiness faded.

'I love another,' he said.
'I know.' She frowned a little
and nodded.

One day he returned.
'I made a mistake,' he said.
'I know.' She smiled and nodded.
'Too late now, too late.'

The inner man

Their marriage was a perfect union of trust and understanding. They shared everything – except his desk drawer, which, through the years, remained locked.

One day, curiosity overcame her. Prised open, there was – nothing.

'But why?' she asked, confused and ashamed.

'I needed a space of my own,' he replied sadly.

Fantasy

The next group of mini-sagas are fantasies from writers who let their imaginations run free.

'For Frank'

Prepared though they were, the first sight of the alien was still a shock.

Seventeen feet tall, and pyramid shaped. Three heads, two of which were under its arms. One square eye at the end of each prehensile toe. But you can't help liking someone who wears a pink bow-tie.

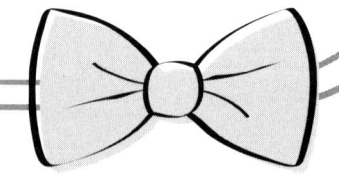

Happily ever after

Doing the dishes, she daydreamed back to the first time she'd met him, before their dreams fell apart, before she learned that you can never change the one you marry, no matter what they promise. Back to when she found him on that lily pad, and gave that fateful kiss.

Time warp

The woman pushed her pram along the path. Her daughter came running to meet her and peered into the pram, in amazement.

'Who is she?' she asked warily.

'This is you when you were six months old.'

Her daughter just kept staring into her own eyes.

At noon

I had been bothered with phone calls before but none really frightening. The phone rang. I picked it up and a man's voice said, 'Time stops at noon.'

I was worried and decided to go down town. I returned at noon and entered the room, entered the room, entered the …

Oops!

> The next pair of mini-sagas is about big mistakes.

A relief to all concerned

'I must go. It's very urgent.'
'More important than I am?'
she asked.
He left hurriedly.
'I never want to see you again,'
she screamed after him.

A door banged.
'Harry,' she called. 'Come back.'
Silence.
A cistern flushed.
A door opened.
'What the hell's the matter now?'
he said.

Who cares?

Maud got up, drew the curtains and groped her way to the bathroom.

'Carer's late today,' she thought.

Jane finally managed to turn right into Ashley Close, saw the curtains.

'She'll be OK. She can have a bath tomorrow.'

She drove off.

Maud is worried, the water is getting cold.

Riddles

> The mini-sagas in this group have a secret meaning and it is your job to work out who or what they are really about.

Homecoming

'Good to have you back, son,'
the old man said.
   'Nice to be back.'
   'You've had a rough time.'
   The eyes clouded with guilt.
'Hope you don't think I let you down.'
   The younger shook his head.
   'You warned me, Dad. But it
wasn't the nails. It was the kiss.'

Life and numbers

Once upon a time there was just Me.
I soon realised there were three of us,
then gradually four.
At last there were just the two of us.
All at once four of us.
Suddenly just the two of us again.
Now there is only Me as in the beginning.

The night of the monkey

The monkey came.

It smoked her fags. Ate her food. Threw up in the sink. Lost her shoes. Drank her booze. Stole her purse. Bought a kebab. Kidnapped some bloke. Re-parked her car. Trashed her room. Swapped her brain for cottonwool.

Next day she swore – she'd never drink again.

Dreams come true

These two mini-sagas are about hopes and dreams that sometimes come true.

A dream in an orphanage

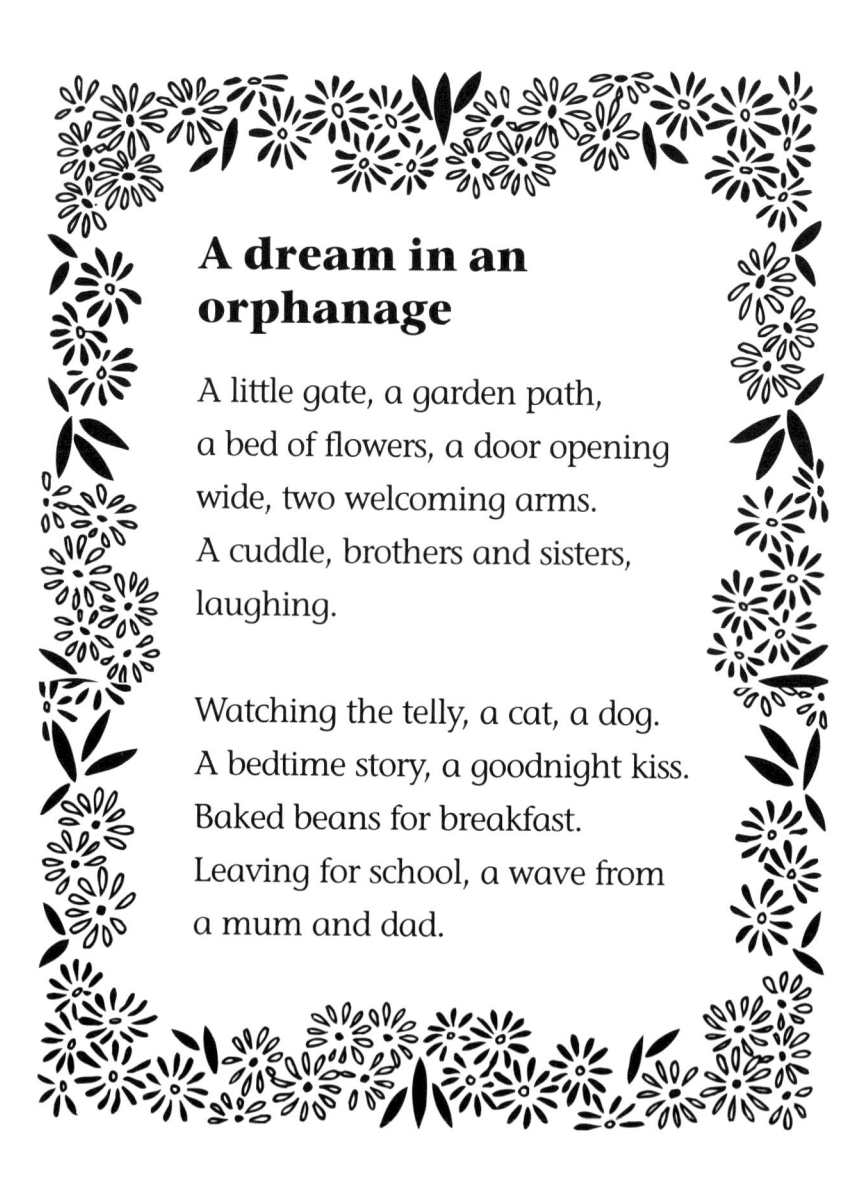

A little gate, a garden path,
a bed of flowers, a door opening
wide, two welcoming arms.
A cuddle, brothers and sisters,
laughing.

Watching the telly, a cat, a dog.
A bedtime story, a goodnight kiss.
Baked beans for breakfast.
Leaving for school, a wave from
a mum and dad.

To live again

I remember my mother.
I was five when my eyes began
to grow dim.
River blindness grows fast.
I grew too and had a little daughter.
She helped me see.
One day white men came to our
village and gave me my sight.
I saw my mother in her face.

Sting in the tail

… Or is that Sting in the Tale? These next two mini-sagas have great last lines.

Pain in a bottle

'Don't you ever cry?' yelled the bully.

The boy remained silent.

'Empty your pockets, and I mean empty.'

The boy obliged.

'Hanky – ugh! keep that. Chocolate, pen, notebook – ha, you're a trainspotter. Seven pounds ten pence – what's in this bottle then?'

'Those are the tears I've cried,' replied the boy.

The death touch

When a daughter went away to college, she reluctantly left her plants and her goldfish in her mother's care. Once the daughter telephoned and her mother confessed that the plants and the goldfish had died. There was a prolonged silence. Finally, in a small voice, the daughter asked, 'How's Dad?'

Writing a mini-saga

Morning.

Blank paper faces me. This is more difficult than I thought. Time passes. Think of a subject. Reject it. Then another. Pause for a cup of coffee. Still no inspiration. Foolish of me to try and write something like this.

Lunch time. Food for thought? Just four more words.

Answers to the Riddles!

Homecoming
The son is Jesus, the father is God. The nails refer to the crucifixion and the kiss is the one which Judas used to betray him.

Life and numbers
You could find different ways to explain this mini-saga. It is about change in a family. First, the writer is born and realises she has a mother and father (3); then a brother or sister comes along (4); then she is married (2); they have 2 children (4); the children leave home (2); then her partner dies (1). There are clues that her children may have been twins.

The night of the monkey
The monkey is the effects of alcohol.

Acknowledgements

Lifetime on p.4 written by Jackie Currie, Bidford-on-Avon
To love forever on p.5 written by Ulla Corkill, Peel
The inner man on p.6 written by Christine M. Banks
'For Frank' on p.8 written by David Brazier, Bembridge
Happily ever after on p.9 written by M.L. Watts, London N1
Time warp on p.10 written by Rita Cullingford, Eastleigh
At noon on p.11 written by Stuart Calder, Dundee
A relief to all concerned on p.13 written by Elizabeth Georgiana Bolton, Ombersley
Who cares? on p.14 written by P. Woodhouse, Sutton
Homecoming on p.16 written by Roger Woddis
Life and numbers on p.17 written by Frances Politzer, Trumpington
The night of the monkey on p.18 written by Claire Evans, Godalming
A dream in an orphanage on p.20 written by B.N. Pople, London SW3
To live again on p.21 written by Christine Duncan, Exmouth
Pain in a bottle on p.23 written by Bett Wareing, Preston
The death touch on p.24 written by Dawn Hunt, Stafford
Writing a mini-saga on p.25 written by Ian Laing, Llandudno Junction